The Swan Song of Vaudeville:
Tales and Takes

The Swan Song of
Vaudeville:
Tales and Takes

Alan Ziegler

Zoo Press

Zoo Press • P.O. Box 3528 • Omaha, Nebraska • 68103
Printed in the United States of America

Cover art: Everett Shinn, "The Monologist," 1910, pastel
on paper; The Roland P. Murdock Collection, Wichita Art
Museum, Wichita, Kansas

Cover design by Janice Clark of Good Studio © 2004
www.goodstudio.com

Distributed to the trade by The University of Nebraska Press
Lincoln, Nebraska • 68588 • www.nebraskapress.unl.edu

Library of Congress Cataloging-in-Publication Data

Ziegler, Alan.
  The swan song of Vaudeville : tales and takes / Alan Ziegler.
      p. cm.
  ISBN 1-932023-19-4 (pbk. : alk. paper)
  I. Title.

PS3576.I29S93 2004
818'.54--dc22

                                                        2004019915

zoo28

First Edition

Acknowledgments

Some of these pieces (or earlier versions of them) appeared in *The Paris Review, The New Yorker, The Party Train: A Collection of North American Prose Poetry* (New Rivers Press), *The American Poetry Review, Sun, The Ardis Anthology of New American Poetry, The Village Voice*, and *So Much To Do* (Release Press).

The author wishes to express his gratitude to Richard Howard, for this and all.

always for Erin

Table of Contents

V

VI

VII

Vamp Until Ready: A Note on the Tales and Takes of Alan Ziegler

It is altogether appropriate for Alan Ziegler, whose accents are frequently those of Fields, of Jolson, of Sophie Tucker, to invoke the shtick of Vaudeville, with its abiding melancholy under, and even within, the sniggers and yaks, its ubiquitous cruelty, and its surreal overtones (weren't the Marx Brothers a great favorite of Andre Breton?), as we so easily recollect from our youthful satisfaction in antics of this order:

First Comic: Why are you bandaged and limping and
                black-and-blue all over?
Second Comic: My wife hit me with the tomatoes.
First Comic: How could she do so much damage?
Second Comic: These tomatoes were in a can.

For these texts of Ziegler are bequeathed by a Shame Culture (Bruno Schultz, say) rather than a Guilt Culture (Kafka), and there is always, therefore, a certain normative Drang rather than the excruciating Sturm to which we have become so habituated in our commitment to the world of the Blank Czech. Of course there are overlaps, particularly in the poetry of conjugal life, which Ziegler is especially given to, or taken by, as he would say, in his Schwanengesang: these prose poems are strikingly Schubertian, indeed, in their economy, their easy invocation of the pleasures of abjection, the Schadenfreude of stifling interiors (Washington Heights Biedermeier) and equally murderous exteriors as well—the street-smarts that turn so rapidly to superhighway pile-ups...

For I guess we must call these "easy pieces" (to abide by my musical identification) prose poems, though literature in English has never welcomed the genre with any confidence. The poet himself employs a more useful nomenclature with "tales and takes," and leaves it to his introducer to assert that the swan songs of Vaudeville are indeed poems for all their leering prose, their funnyman's slap and tickle, their barker's spiel outside the freakshow of modern religion (don't miss "God's Will" in what follows), modern education (ibid "The Encyclopedia of Trees"), modern love (ibid "All of Me"); one reason I know that Ziegler's performances are poems is that the language, the voice has been altogether honed to memorable speech, Auden's working title for modern poetry. The form (to speak boldly) of these "takes" (the photographic figure imposes itself along with the musical one) is that kind of furious improvisation which follows upon the discovery that we are isolated not only from each other but from ourselves at other times; their value is in the virtuosity of the vamping, and it will last until Living destroys them (the deceit of "mutual understanding" will do as much, and the revelation that everyone is a multiple personality corresponding to the possibilities of Being to be found in each of us), and we must improvise some more. At which time Ziegler will have proved to be our man.

—Richard Howard

I

In the City of Mystery

In the city of mystery the road signs are changed hourly. You never know who will show up at your door with flowers. Or a knife.

The movie theater skips the first and last reels. The newspaper puts all the names on page one, and the stories minus names on the inside pages.

Each morning you find footprints in your yard; every afternoon there is fog; in the evening a wailing comes from just over the ridge.

The door to the judge's chambers says *Crater*, and the office at the airport says *Earhart*.

Lovers turn their backs on you, and when they come around you don't recognize them. Strangers leap into your arms at the supermarket.

You awaken each morning after a night of dull dreams eager to start the day.

The Guest

You are lost and knock on the nearest door to ask directions. There's a crowd, a party going on. You're about to apologize for interrupting, but everyone at the party treats you as if your arrival has been eagerly anticipated. This woman embracing you—do you know her? And this man slapping your back—is he an old roommate from school? They are listening to music you love, and offer you shrimps with lobster sauce, your favorite.

Is this in your honor? Did you do something worthy without being aware of it? You decide to relax and enjoy; why analyze and maybe spoil it? You sit back, and one by one they come to you. "It was nothing," you hear yourself saying—at least you are telling the truth.

Later, a teary woman makes her way through the crowd. She calls you inconsiderate and curses you. You don't know how to respond, so you say nothing. She leaves, and everyone is quiet. The host comes over and says softly with a tinge of bitterness, "You know, you shouldn't have ignored her all night. It was hard enough for her to come. Sometimes you can be such a bastard."

Lonely

You walk the late-afternoon streets.

A cop enters a coffee shop to get something to-go, leaving his partner outside. The partner paces, lonely, wondering what's taking so long.

The faint moon is lonely in the blue sky.

A woman in a pink dress walks a dog. The dog is lonely for other dogs and tugs whenever he sees one. The problem of this dog's loneliness cannot be solved by the company of the woman in pink.

The woman in pink is lonely. The companionship of the dog helps, but is not enough.

A beggar posted at a subway exit gets lonely between trains.

"In the Wee Small Hours of the Morning" wails from the window of a cheap hotel.

The sun sets, and in rooms where lights do not go on, lonely people sit in the dark.

The moon is covered by a single, lonely cloud; they will soon drift apart.

You weave among them all, eyes open, breathing, listening, keeping your composure, not letting them know that you know.

Somewhere a Phone Is Ringing

Somewhere a phone is ringing on a hot summer night. You don't take note of it until the tenth or twelfth ring. After the twentieth or so, you wonder how long the caller will let it ring.

Still ringing when you go to bed at 1:30 a.m., receding as you ease behind the scrim of sleep. Each time you wake, you determine that the rings have not entered your dreams but are present in the night.

You think:

Perhaps, a man is calling his ex-girlfriend. He brandishes the phone as she cowers in the corner of her studio apartment. If she lifts the receiver to yell "Hang up!" he will shout her name and be back in her life.

Maybe she's not home and his desperate ringing is for naught, but how can he be sure? If she is there and he hangs up he will have lost her forever.

Maybe he knows she's not home but she has a parrot that will drive her crazy with telephone ringing for the next forty years.

Maybe he's not home. He punched in her number and left his apartment. He's with another woman, getting off on the image of his old girlfriend cowering in the corner.

You choose a more felicitous scenario:

Lovers separated by the continent, entwined in the ringing of their love in each other's ears.

At 8:30 a.m. the phone is ringing as you eat breakfast. It is all right by you.

For So Long

Late Sunday night you emerge, carrying the remains of a wretched weekend wrapped in a large brown paper bag dripping bacon grease, brimming with tin cans half-full of concentrated soup and stuffed with crumpled paper.

A crazed dog challenges you for your bounty. You hold your ground and refuse his drooling mouth, stand pat against his damp snarling. You want the dog to ask you nicely—whimper, heel.

The dog snorts and turns away. You hold the bag out to him and kick his hairy snout.

Now the dog goes berserk with hunger and anger. The rancid smorgasbord you clutch will no longer satisfy him. It's a piece of you he wants.

He salvages your weekend the way he looks at you, the way no one has looked at you for so long.

In This Bar

In this bar you no longer drink. The bartender has stopped approaching you.

In this bar you no longer talk. People have ceased asking questions.

In this bar you no longer write. Your life is an open book of blank pages.

In this bar what you do is remember. Your mind makes paths through the past.

In this bar occasionally you make with a song that keeps the crowds coming.

Untangling

Last night I spent four minutes untangling the wires connected to a pair of headphones I put in a drawer alongside assorted wired devices.

I do not recall spending any time tangling the wires before I closed the drawer.

I have spent several hours of my life untangling wires, and I have never consciously tangled anything.

It must be *something* I do.

★

I save the last cup of coffee in the pot to reheat tomorrow morning because I am incapable of making a decent cup of coffee until I have had my first cup of coffee.

I really need that second cup.

★

I have discovered the formula for happiness, the roadmap to contentment, and the recipe for good living. Unfortunately, I am terrible at following directions.

★

I tell the story counterclockwise, getting younger until "This is where I came in."

I continue. Not much to do now. I tire of being asked, "Who the hell are *you*?"

If this thing ever kicks out of reverse gear, they'll find out.

Yes sir, they are in for some surprise, given what I know now.

★

I discovered I could fly when a truck backfired and I fled with the pigeons, scampering then lifting off, fueled by surprise and companionship.

I wonder if this is a one-shot deal. But the only way to find out would be to land.

II

Taking Stock

The supply room is empty, and no one knows when the next delivery is due.

No one can remember the last shipment or who ordered it, only that we were well-supplied for a long time.

We call every number in the Rolodex and say, "We have none left. Please bring more."

Some are sympathetic, some blasé, others downright rude. No one says for sure when we can expect a delivery.

I say, "At least we have one another," but the others are gone. Just me amidst empty closets, empty chairs next to empty desks.

I can barely see in the twilight and turn on a lamp; the bulb gives a final flicker and dies. There is simply no point in looking for another one.

The sun, too, runs out.

I am left with a night's supply of darkness. I shall make it last.

Blanket of Hair

The barber leans against the shoulder of his fifth customer on a Tuesday afternoon. He pretends the contact is inadvertent, a byproduct of maneuvering into the optimal snipping angle. But artistry is not the issue, he is snipping as much air as hair. He is bone weary.

The barber promises himself that he will never cut another hair if only he can somehow get through this day without crumpling to the floor or being berated by a customer who detects hair larceny through the hand-held rearview mirror.

The barber rallies off the customer's shoulder and blessedly finds himself back in rhythm, instinctively clipping and snipping in all the right places. The customer will go home and someone will say "Nice haircut" and mean it.

As the barber sweeps the floor at the end of the day, he is struck by the cruelty of this revival. If he had completely broken down, he could have fled the shop screaming, winding up on some distant shore where his soul could reincarnate.

When the barber has swept all the hair into one pile, he scoops it in his arms and rocks it like a baby. He carries the pile to his room behind his shop and lays it on the blanket of hair on his bed, hair that never gets grayer or thinner than the day it was shorn. He flings himself on the pile.

Symphonic Diaspora

The Philharmonic can't agree on which park the concert is scheduled for. The first chairs bicker, and the conductor does the baton dance, trying to find the melody.

The conductor can't tame the cacophony. He would settle for dissonance, but his baton has become a blind talisman.

The Philharmonic Balkanizes; the conductor snaps his baton like a wishbone.

Weeks later, on a new carnival block, farther east than most people have ever ventured, symphonic blues seep from newly-painted storefronts.

Woolworths Parakeets

Hundreds of Woolworths are closing and thousands of generic parakeets will be released on noon of the final day. Scrawny blue-and-green ten-dollar birds will scatter in downtown Las Vegas, uptown New York City, and suburban Lynbrook. They will be freed from their group homes, where they sleep leaning on each other like passengers on a midnight train in India. These are not the cream of the exotic bird crop; they are bred for volume, their markup too low to keep Woolworths in flight. If you see one in your neighborhood, coax it home with seeds and love. Let it fly around the house, offer it food off your plate, teach it the words you've longed for someone to say to you, and love it as you love the America that once you knew.

The Shepherd's Lament

I am no longer able to do well by my flock. Frankly, they bore me. I wave my staff this way and that; they double-take and follow, but with increasing irritation.

The dog covers for me, yipping and nudging. When he looks to me for guidance I nod *over there* while I search the sky over *here*.

I cede him the staff. He is in charge now, and he is having a ball.

If he and his descendants play their cards right, this will all be theirs.

As for my offspring: things could go either way.

The Swan Song of Vaudeville

I would see her silhouette sometimes through the shaded window of her room over the marquee.

Heart fluttering, I would go in and perform. Vaudeville was getting old, but I was young. Three years with the man in the bear suit, till he retired. By then I had developed enough characters to go out on my own, on the road for months at a time. But always back to the theater under the marquee under her room.

On nights when her light was off and the shade up, I would peek from behind the curtain until the house lights went down, searching the audience for her.

One night, during my ventriloquism bit, as the dummy sang "Love's Old Sweet Song" while I swallowed fire, I thought I heard an orgasm from above.

I transfigured the spit-take into high art, hilarious to everyone in the house except me.

That night my performance vaulted the walls of time, and my closing number is often considered to be the swan song of vaudeville.

III

Ghostly

I feel a tapping on my shoulder. I live alone. No one else has keys. My heart races as if trying to flee to a safer body. But I am startled for only an instant. I turn around and, sure enough, it's merely that ghost. He always shows up when I feel most alive, which for a long time meant infrequent visits. Lately I've come to expect him at least once a week.

He never uses fancy theatrics to frighten me. No creaking footsteps from the closet or lightning bolts piercing the bedroom wall. No howls or shrieks, no low moans or clanking chains. "I'm not too good on the audiovisuals," he once explained after trying to project hand-shadow ghouls onto the wall.

Sometimes he hides behind a chair and emits a feeble "Boo!"—and then, "Don't be scared, it's only me." Once, I discovered the word "demon" written in what I thought was blood on the front door. It turned out to be a jelly smear from one of the doughnuts he'd brought as a treat. He apologized and then scrubbed the door clean.

Tonight it's just a tap on the shoulder. He shrugs, as if to apologize for startling me. We sit for a while, until I forget why I was so cheerful. He has a smoky presence, vaguely shaped into limbs and facial features—nothing I could grab hold of, though God knows I've been afraid even to try.

Three days later, I return home from work feeling chipper. He is lying on the couch and rises with a start when I close the door. "Huh!...Oh, it's only you," he says.

He seems weary, even more translucent than usual. I make some coffee, and we drink it quietly. He dunks his cruller and lets it dissolve in the blackness. The smoke from his cigarette looks like ghost-children wandering in the air.

"Anything wrong?" I ask.

He stares at the cold coffee. "There's something about living I'm beginning to miss," he says at last. "I can't remember what it is, not for the life of me." For the first time I think I see a flicker of a smile. He shrugs, and his borders undulate, giving the impression of a full-bodied fidget.

"Please go on," I say softly.

A bolt of lightning zips across the window, and he looks admiringly at it. "I thoroughly appreciated deadness," he says. "Now I feel almost nostalgic for the days when people disliked me for who I was, not for what I represent."

I reach out to touch him, forgetting how scared I've been to do that. He pulls away, though a coolness in my palm makes me think I might have grazed him. "Sorry," I say. "Only trying to help. You're fading away, pal."

"A throbbing where my bones used to be," he murmurs.

"Maybe you're coming back to life."

"I don't believe in that crap," he whispers as he merges with the last puff from his cigarette. Soon that too is gone, and I am alone in the room, which vibrates as if reacting to a tremor from someplace below. Traffic, no doubt.

Elegy

I float over her life as her voice rises like smoke escaping an explosion, weaker as it wisps into a whisper. But still I hear it, I hear what she is saying: wounded words like birds shot in flight on a stretcher of wind. The ghostwriting grazes the sky, feeding on the air I breathe as I drown to the ground.

In Continuum

Now, while the time since your death is still counted in weeks, I'll be walking along and there, just beyond my eyes' ability to distinguish faces, I'll see someone who looks like you, and for a few milliseconds my brain will form your face.

At first it was a little unnerving, but I've come to look forward to and treasure those milliseconds, and I will mourn them when they are gone.

The Night I Couldn't Find My Arm

I wake in the middle of the night and can't find my left arm. Not draped over my wife or squished under my chest. I panic for a few groggy seconds.

There it is: by my side, too heavy to lift.

I remember hearing that prisoners in concentration camps were sometimes forced to sleep in such confined spaces that their whole bodies fell asleep while their minds remained conscious.

I muffle a scream into the pillow as I shake my arm awake, breathing rapidly until I can once again embrace my wife.

God's Will

It is literally true: God created the heavens and the earth, the waters and the living creatures, in six days. He rested on the seventh.

God really liked that seventh day, and continued to rest on His laurels. He *meant* to improve Earth, but after that first week He mostly let the free will He had bestowed run its course.

He did some standard maintenance and a few adjustments here and there, which left a lot of time to think about the two concepts that even He never really understood:

What preceded His own existence; even if truly nothing existed before Him, what exactly *is* nothing?

And, He had trouble with *infinity*. He knew He ruled all He could see, but how could He know for sure if He really saw all.

The two questions were entwined: If some force had created God, then maybe it had also created a place He wasn't privy to.

These questions occupied millennia of meditation, to little avail. But it made God quite sympathetic to those who devoted their lives to pure thought, such as theologians, poets, and sportswriters.

God felt warmly toward people of all religions. Whenever anyone mentioned "God," He knew they were referring to Him, since He had done it all, though often under an alias. God thoroughly enjoyed religious services, constantly scanning synagogues, churches, and mosques. He monitored individual prayers and kept a to-do list in His prodigious mind.

But whenever He was about to get back to work, those two bugaboos—nothingness and infinity—would get the better of Him, and He would continue His R&R: rest and rumination.

His calendar remained a month of Sundays.

Regret gnawed at Him. Maybe if He had worked on that original seventh day, when He was on a roll, He might have created better methods than war and illness to provide constant changes in the cast of characters. (Though God had to admit that He was hooked on the drama; He was the supreme channel surfer.)

One day He really would need to get back to work; in the meantime, what could those who scorned Him do to Him? One of His favorite expressions that humans had used their free will to compose was: "So, they'll call me *pisher*," meaning roughly: *All they can do is call me a name.* Whenever anyone took God's name in vain, or railed against Him, He would think: "Go ahead, call me *pisher*," sometimes adding, "You *stoonard*."

Then one day that infinity thing came to bite God on his divine ass. Somewhere out there *was* another God, who had created another heaven and fruitful planet. Could this be God's sibling, or maybe a superior breed of God? Now those damned questions weren't theoretical.

God learned about this other God through His all-knowingness. How this knowledge came to Him, He didn't know. He just knew.

He also knew that the other God had not rested on the seventh day. This God kept on working. This God had found a way to keep suffering in the abstract. On His planet all were artists: they wept, they laughed, and they appreciated suffering, experiencing it only on stage and screen, on canvas and the page. On His planet, heaven was a verifiable fact, so death was approached mournfully but without terror.

The astronomers created by the other God had found out about Earth and the physical suffering on it. In their prayers they implored their God to save the Earth from the legacy of neglect. Their God responded by making this proposal to the lazy God: "Clean up your act, make peace with the people of the Earth, or face my wrath. Because I can do more than call you *pisher*, you *dumbkopf*."

Earth's God was not sure who had the leverage. Maybe the activist God wasn't as tough as He was hard-working. But since obviously Earth God didn't understand *everything*, He would take no chances. So, He did some divine genetic engineering, creating brilliant doctors, scientists, philosophers, and teachers of the arts. He smote phony preachers and imbued those who remained with an unimpeachable aura of credibility. The quality of life improved exponentially.

It was hard, nonstop work, but He rather came to enjoy it.

One day He realized that at some point He had stopped being aware of the other God. He was off the hook; life on Earth was far from idyllic, but it wasn't so baffling. He could rest again, albeit briefly and occasionally.

On His first day of rest in ages, God snapped to attention. It occurred to Him that if He was as all-powerful and all-knowing as He had always believed Himself to be, it was possible that He himself had planted the awareness of a superior God into His all-knowingness as a means of self-motivation. Humans had used their free will to fill shelves of Barnes and Noble with such gimmicks.

But if He remained at rest, He would forever grapple with holy doubt, waiting for the other cosmic shoe to drop. To play it safe, God vowed eternal vigilance and assistance. And they all lived happily ever after.

IV

Love At First Sight

It was a novelty-store and he went in just for the novelty of it. She was in front of the counter, listening to the old proprietor say: "I have here one of those illusion paintings, a rare one. You either see a beautiful couple making love, or a skull. They say this one was used by Freud himself on his patients—if at first sight you see the couple, then you are a lover of life and love. But if you focus on the skull first, you're closely involved with death, and there's not much hope for you."

With that, the proprietor unwrapped the painting. They both hesitated, looked at the picture, then at each other. They both saw the skull. And have been together ever since.

All of Me

You said it's so quiet when I'm gone, so I left my tongue behind for you.

"What's this slimy little pest doing here, and how do I shut it up?"

You complained you had no one to talk to, so I left an ear. Ashtray.

You got horny, you purred, so I left my penis.

Fine for a while, till you found it redundant and somewhat limited.

Then: my hands to touch you, feet to follow you.

"All of you," you said you wanted, all of me.

Now your room is fully equipped, yet you complain of the clutter and wonder what you ever saw in me.

Answering the Mail

A woman opens her mailbox and discovers a package. Inside is a living, breathing miniature version of the mailman, which reminds the woman that she did not tip him at Christmas. She would gladly make it up to the mailman, especially considering his plight, but she has only a half-dollar on hand and is afraid it would be a burden in his present condition.

She asks the mailman what has happened, and he replies, "Every morning I tremble as I approach your little house. I see exquisite anticipation on your face as I come up the walk, only to watch you turn away from me and bless my offerings. I leave your doorstep with the thought of your glorious fingers gently unwrapping these garments and reaching in. I have grown jealous of the things I bring, so I have become one of them."

The woman considers this as she looks down at this delivery, which looks back with questions written all over it.

She takes her mail inside and composes a detailed response.

The Encyclopedia of Trees

A new tree has grown behind the house this morning, and I haven't the foggiest how to care for it.

I had thought I sensed something brewing: Above a barren circle in the yard, birds kept returning to hover, like musicians looking for their instruments.

This morning while shaving I noticed the leaves, and I ran outside into the glaring sun. The birds fit like keys.

Please come back with the encyclopedia of trees and read to me in the new shade.

Swan

As I sulked, a swan came out of the river. I told her all about you, pointing to where you lay in the sun, eyes closed, pink sweater beside you. I mentioned your eyes and how they matched the grass.

The swan started toward you. I told her you wanted to be left alone. She turned and eased back down into the river.

Why, she hardly knew you—yet she understood so quickly it put me to shame.

Our Days

Longing for you I walk the early morning streets: across 96th to Broadway, where I take the Métro (it's so clean) to St.-Germain.

A clochard shines my shoes and I toss him a coin, gold and silver gleaming in the autumn sun. At 34th and Fifth I gaze up at the Eiffel Tower as businessmen hurry by and tourist-lovers linger with dewy eyes.

As I span the Seine on the Brooklyn Bridge, it starts to rain. I stop for a *café noir* with a bagel and shmear, flirt with the toy poodle held by an old woman on the straw chair at the next table.

The rain dissipates and the vast grey canopy of the sky turns silver, then gold, and I want to shout *Je comprends, je comprends,* but everyone already knows that from my face, for I am thinking of tonight, when we will discuss our days as we dine, gazing across the vast table of bounty.

So Much To Do

Could you come over here? There are a few things I want to go over. For example, your naked arms.

Particularly above the elbows. I don't see much of your arms now that the weather is cold. Not that they are never there for me, but I have been conditioned to focus along the center of your bare body and slightly to the left and right. At some of the best moments your arms are completely out of sight, around me, drawing me closer to your face. Ah, your face, I could spend hours there, but not right now. Above the elbows, the backs of your knees, your ankles, your softly curved calves—especially your calves, I want to wrap around them the way the tops of your socks do. Also, the back of your neck (one of the most underrated parts of the body)—a kiss there just hard enough not to tickle. I want so much of you, dream-volumes of flesh, hair, nails. The third rib from the bottom on the left side, I've been meaning to get there for six weeks. All the neglected outskirts, acquaintances on the peripheries of the intimate friendships I have formed with the flashier parts of your body. Those special friends will not be jealous, they will understand why I pass them over—indeed, they will share in the good fortunes of their neighbors. And they know I will return home before I sleep.

V

The Last Refuge

We wave flags as the parade passes by.

From the furious looks on the marchers' faces, we realize we have the wrong flags.

Now we lead the parade.

Only it's not a parade any more as the marchers give chase, but by a strategic use of back alleys, loading docks, and fruit carts, we wind up at the rear of the mob.

We join in yelling "Get those guys, teach 'em a lesson," and escalate with "Kill the bastards, string 'em up."

With increasing fury, we weave our way toward the front, vengeance in our souls.

From Our Corresponent on the Scene

The ventriloquists' civil war has turned ugly.

Outside a club, a man in a midnight blue tuxedo leans over the smoldering remains of a wooden figure sheathed in tattered pieces of the same blue cloth.

Nearby, a man in a white suit lies, limp, a goofy grin spanning his throat, which cackles as the blood gurgles out.

Other Voices

I overhear other people's imaginary voices.

Sometimes, when I have a chance, I do the voices' biddings. I expect no thanks and get none.

One day, I fulfill an elegantly violent request from a voice speaking to the woman in 9A, only to meet her wrath.

I realize I misunderstood: it's hard when there are so many voices. I'll have to concentrate more, even if it means ignoring my own voices. That's the kind of good neighbor I am.

Victimless Crime

You come home, find your possessions gone. You sigh and go to bed.

You wake with a start, bed stolen from under your nose. Weary so weary, you go back to sleep. You'll investigate tomorrow.

You reawaken to a slap of chill wind. Someone has made off with the south wall. Overcoat on blanket, you curl into a sad question mark.

You dream of marching in a distant war. When you wake again, you are a double amputee.

By morning there is no trace of you.

Caught

Strange that the woman walking close behind you wears a raincoat and galoshes in the sun; you don't recall a prediction of rain. You glance again and detect something menacing about the way she carries her umbrella.

You turn down a side street. She turns. You slip into an alley. She follows. You about-face, poised to parry umbrella with keys. You mirror glare with glare. "What is it you want?" you demand.

"At last," she says. "Your disguise is clever, but not clever enough."

Her voice is as familiar as a coat which kept you warm all winter but which you lost somewhere along the way. Your disguise *is* clever, but not so clever as hers.

VI

For One of Your Smiles...

An infant crawls away from home and lies down next to a river. He sleeps through puberty. When he wakes up and looks at his body, he realizes his absence must have caused a lot of pain. Fortunately for him, he is an adolescent and doesn't much care.

He falls back to sleep and reawakens middle-aged. Now the thought of his loved ones' grief makes him dizzy and he passes out.

He comes to. He is old and needs to stretch, to walk, to wander—the same sensations that got him into this predicament.

Somehow he makes his way back home. His mother sits on the porch swing weeping. She is unspeakably old, yet she cries with joy when she sees him: "My baby, my baby, you have returned."

He kneels by her side, and as she runs her hand through his thin white hair, she says, "So many times I've wondered where you were, what you were doing. Tell me everything."

He joins her on the swing, cradles her in his arms, and begins to tell her his dreams.

Finishing Touches

A father and son built a house, something they didn't know much about. But the father needed a place to live, and they enjoyed learning together. The son is staying with the father until they complete the finishing touches.

The ceilings slope, the doorway forces people to enter sideways, and the plumbing necessitates occasional visits to the gas station down the road. But they did it themselves and know they could do it again, better.

The son taught the father the little he knows about cooking. He will eat well, though the menus will be repetitive for now.

Someday the father will meet someone who will put up with sloping ceilings, sideways entrances, and walks to the gas station. Eventually the two of them will move out. This house will be torn down, replaced by something more functional. The father does not think about that now. He thinks about the son's leaving, which he knows is as necessary as his being here has been.

The son sits alone in the living room, staring wearily at the plastered walls while the father makes dinner. As he cooks he sings—a lovely sad old song. He pauses to search among the ingredients on the shelves and to check the two pots on the burners. When he resumes, the son joins in the harmony, off key but on kilter, a couple of hungry guys home for now.

Ties

You're not sure what to say when the man comes to your door and gasps *brother*. You do have a long-lost brother, but this man does not resemble your memory of him. The man's clothes are scuffed, his boots muddy, but his face glows with the bliss of the returning pilgrim. What to say to him? You would not want to reject him only to find out later that he really *is* your brother. But if he is *not* your brother, he must be someone who no longer knows who he is, going from door to door, hoping finally to reach the right door, where his true brother anxiously awaits. You do not want to impede his quest by taking him in as your own brother. For what if you take him in and someday your real brother shows up in need? This is a small house; you and your wife are not what you would call a bighearted couple.

You wife comes home and embraces her long-lost brother. As they reminisce, the house seems even smaller than before, and you long for your brother.

The Family Garden

Standing by my side, she places her arm lovingly around me, and there it remains.

Her arm grows heavy, but I can't bear to ask her to remove it.

Her arm takes root; we are in for the long haul.

Medical authorities are astonished that Siamese twindom can be an acquired characteristic.

It is not unpleasant like this. She always has one free hand with which to assist or please me.

Before long, seeds drop and little arms crop up, blooming into children.

It is truly a family that stays together. Cross one and you answer to all.

But as the roots spread, my insides get pushed around, upsetting the fragile botany, a eutrophication of the soul.

I begin to grow weary and irritable.

I want this place cleaned up.

I want a divorce.

Still, when I see her smiling and the little ones at her knees, I find it hard to tell them.

Lately, though, they too seem troubled. The little ones want to wander, and she has things to do which require two arms.

The nourishment from my soil grows thin.

We all agree: an uprooting is due. We brace for the harvest.

VII

Love Potions and Bitter Pills

One

In a crowd someone laughed. Thinking, incorrectly, it was he, a woman said, "What a sad laugh." He smiled and was about to defend himself when she said, "But there's sweetness in your smile, so there's hope for you."

They went off together and he tried not to laugh. A week later, when the joy was too much, he bellowed. She declared, correctly, "I have changed your life."

Two

"Ah, an imperfect beauty," he said as he noticed the scar that whispered along her upper lip.

Perhaps that horrible moment of shattered glass was worth it after all, she thought.

Then she thought again.

Three

The world seemed to have doubled its offering: his two eyes and two ears were no longer sufficient. Only with their four eyes focused together and four ears tuned to the same frequency could he fully see the beauty in art and the sky, and fully hear the music of symphonies and breezes.

Four

In the past, the best that others could do was to help him forget death, briefly. With her, he could be reminded of death and still love life.

Five

They laughed and frolicked and kissed and nuzzled and ravaged and napped and did it all over again. She said, "They should slap a caption on us: *In happier days*."

Six

The voice on the radio was hysterical. They turned it up until they couldn't make out the words, drowning out the phone and the sirens.

They shut the windows and harmonized in a hymn. Her hands threw scary shadow figures from her past onto the wall. His fist shadows pummeled them.

Seven

He was an incurable optimist until he swallowed her own medicine.

Eight

He believed that her orgasms were authentic, but he started to suspect that she was faking her understanding:
"Oh. Oh. Oh.
"Yes. Yes. Yes.
You poor thing, you!"

Nine

When he told her he loved her, he was caught red-hearted returning to the scene of someone else's crime. She studied him up and down as if cramming for an examination.

Ten

She made him beside himself, and he hardly recognized the man standing next to him.

Each time they parted, he was like a rocking chair she had quickly got out of.

Eleven

He ran away from her in circles, and she ran circles around him.

He surrendered, and she shredded his white flag.

He went limp and bared his jugular, like a vanquished fox, and she snapped at him.

"OK, I give up," he said. "You win. I will fight on."

Twelve

She broke his heart in two. Then she quartered it.

But each portion regenerated.

Now he could run for miles, make love, weep at a sad movie, and still have one cold heart for her.

In a dream of drowning, his life flashed before his eyes. She wasn't there.

Thirteen

On her way out of town for the summer, she dropped by with a bottle of wine. He drove with her and they checked into a motel.

Afterward, he said this was far enough, he'd take the bus back.

This time she was the one who pleaded. This time he was the one who erupted. Anger poured from places in him where he didn't even know he had spouts.

Fourteen

The dust had settled and been swept away. He knew that there was a bulge under a rug somewhere, but frankly he didn't care.

They laughed all evening, and then she closed up on him. He stared at the CD player: *No disc.*

"You know," he said, "you don't have to turn a mountain around to get to the other side."

"God," she replied, "I am so sick of you."

Fifteen

He presented his case with eloquence, even incandescence. He kept at it, on a roll, a tongue/brain parley to beat the band, he felt his saliva effervesce, something chemical was afoot, he was foaming with rhetorical hegemony.

"You're perfectly right," she said, "and perfectly mad," as she eased herself out the door.

Sixteen

He finally got himself to dial her number. "Hello?" she asked, and he hung up, realizing he had no answer.

Seventeen

A night on the town, they agreed, like the old days, might fix it.

They did the cab-dance, to the pool-hall of mirrors. He set up; she broke and ran the table, the balls homing into his pockets. He could barely move when it was finally his turn.

Eighteen

It didn't matter how far they had gone from town. The landscape inside them was the same.

Their first worthwhile moments had been pure lust. Later, nostalgia joined the lust. Now, they talked of old times but ceased making new ones.

Nineteen

She put her finger on his wrist but could find no pulse. They disagreed on the implications.

Twenty

She held on to him long enough to convince him that if he said the right words she wouldn't leave.

He told her, "It's you and me against the world, babe."

She replied, "You are the world to me."

Twenty-One

She grew smaller as she walked away. When she became small enough, he would pick her up, look her in her tiny eyes, and assure her that she was safe with him, he would fix everything. But he lost track of her; she had grown too small for him to help.

Twenty-Two

He watched everyone in the world enter the room, except her. Now, even if she did show up, it might be too crowded. And what was she doing out there all alone?

Twenty-Three

The sadness of the empty dish after the unsatisfying meal. No longing for the food, but the hunger was sorely missed.

Twenty-Four

A new one came along quickly. This one inexperienced, even naive. Oh, his thirst for her.

Twenty-Five

How quick the quenching!

His buried treasure. He broke her with his shovel.

Twenty-Six

The door opened shyly, just a crack, then blossomed into her smile. "Let me tell you," she started, but the sentence was never finished.

Epilogue

When he put on a black robe, she called him "your honor" and abided by his judgments.

When he put on a white smock, she called him "doctor," undressed for him without resistance or shame, and let him heal her.

When he put on a clown suit, she laughed out loud at whatever he did, no matter how painful or sad.

When he put on a gorilla suit, she kept her distance, but threw him food and giggled as he scampered for it.

Now he took everything off. She looked bewildered till he began to cry, and she held him, rocked him gently, singing him to sleep.

Alan Ziegler's books include *So Much to Do* (poems), *The Green Grass of Flatbush* (stories), and *The Writing Workshop, volumes I and II* (on teaching creative writing). His work has appeared in such publications as *The New Yorker* and *The Paris Review*, and his awards include the Word Beat Fiction Book Award (selected by George Plimpton), a New York Foundation for the Arts fellowship, and four PEN-NEA Syndicated Fiction Awards. Ziegler received the Presidential Award for Outstanding Teaching at Columbia University, where he is Professor of Writing and Chair of the School of the Arts Writing Division.